Super Smart Science Series Book 10

This SUPER AWESOME Book Belongs to:

_____

Winner of the Art Competition: Daniella Cohen

Geology:
Earth Composition, Landforms, Rocks & Water

Book 10 of the Super Smart Science Series™
Ages 0-100

Geology: Earth Composition, Landforms, Rocks & Water
ISBN: 978-1-941775-06-6
April Chloe Terrazas, BS University of Texas at Austin.
Copyright © 2014 Crazy Brainz, LLC

Visit us on the web! www.Crazy-Brainz.com
Cover design, illustrations and text by: April Chloe Terrazas

Geology (JEE - OL - O - JEE) is the study of how the earth was formed and what it is made of.

Rocks, mountains, rain, snow, and more!

A geologist (JEE - OL - O - JIST) is a person who is an expert in geology.

You will be a geologist soon!

Earth Composition

(KOM - PUH - ZISH - UN)

Earth is made of 4 main layers:

1) **Inner core** (IN - R KOR)
2) **Outer core** (OUT - R KOR)
3) **Mantle** (MAN -TL)
4) **Crust** (KRUST)

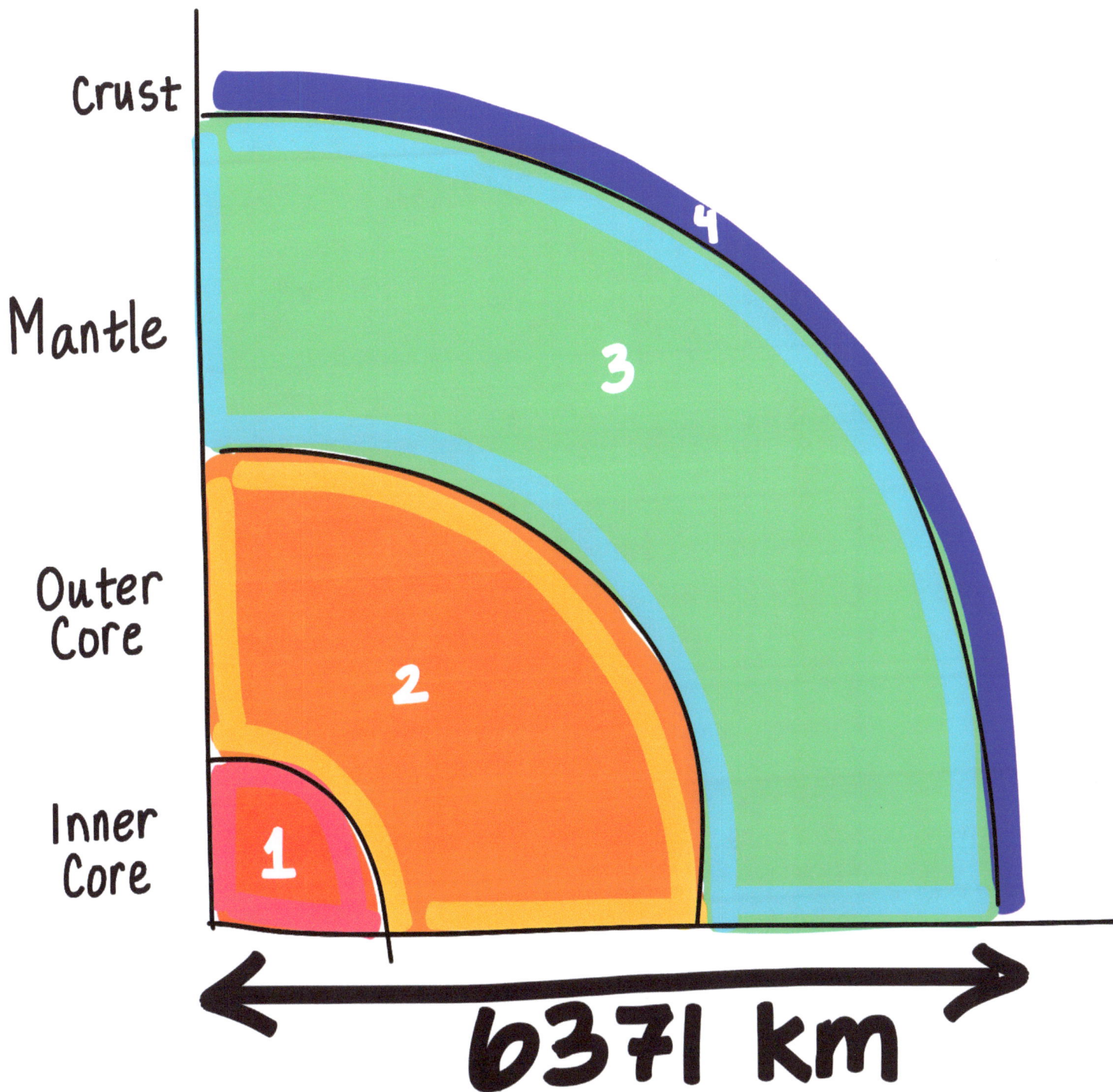

Crust

Mantle

Outer Core

Inner Core

6371 km

The distance from the center of the earth to the surface of the earth is 6,371 kilometers!

(KIL - OM - EH - TRZ)

Driving at 100 kilometers per hour, it would take over 60 hours to reach the center of the earth!

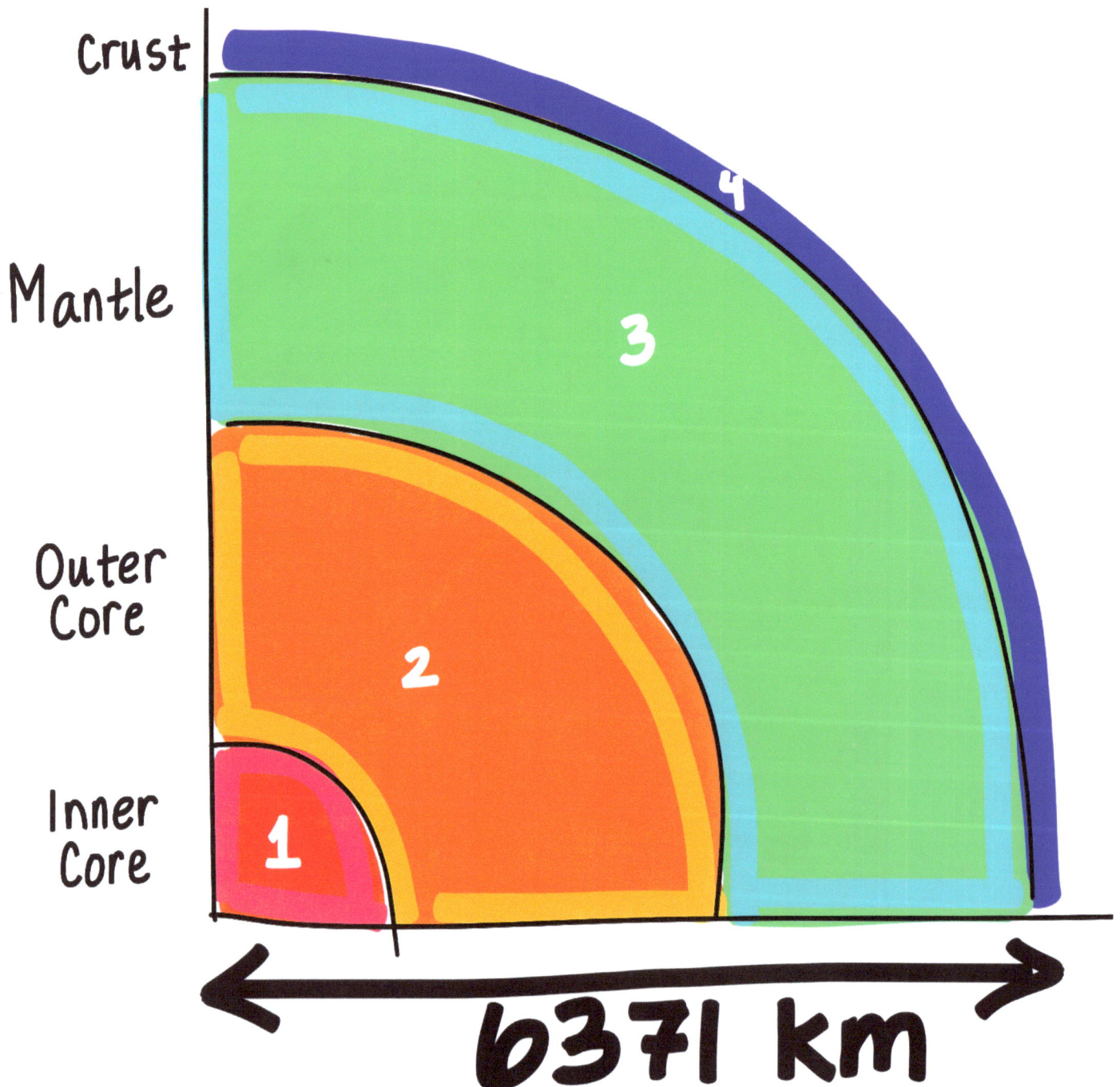

Crust

Mantle

Outer Core

Inner Core

1

2

3

4

6371 km

The core of the earth
(the inner core + outer core)
is made almost entirely of metal.

Temperatures in the inner core
reach 5,000 degrees celsius!
(that's 9,000 degrees Fahrenheit!)

The mantle is the largest part
of the earth and consists
of very hot, solid rock.

The crust is the outer layer
of the earth. It consists of the
continental (KON - TIN - EN - TUL) crust
-covered by land,
and oceanic (O - SHE - AN - IK) crust
-covered by sea.

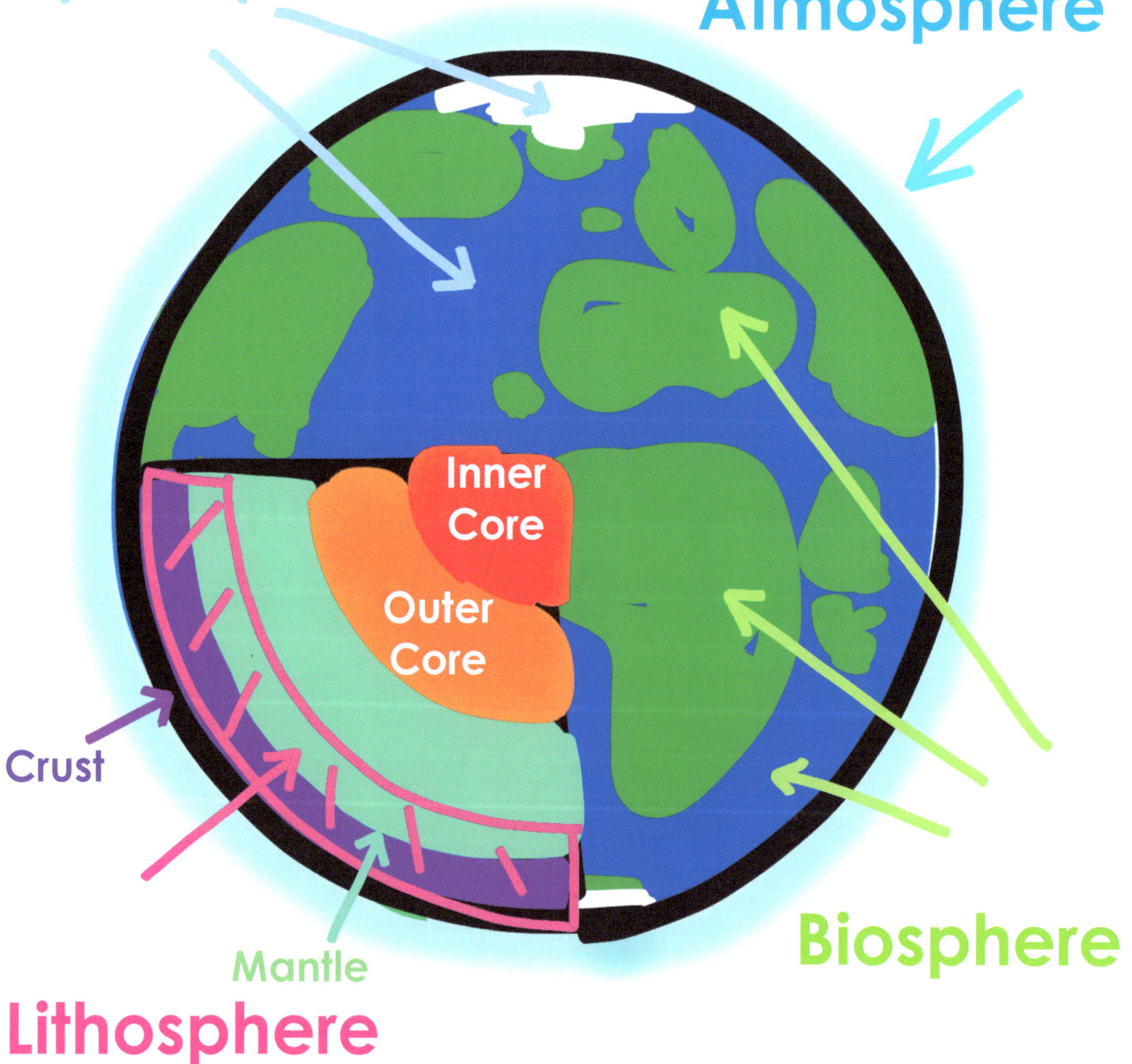

Spheres (SFEERS)

The 4 spheres of the earth interact with each other.

Hydrosphere

Atmosphere

Inner Core

Outer Core

Crust

Mantle

Lithosphere

Biosphere

The hydropshere (HI - DRO - SFEER) is earth's water in solid (ice), liquid (water) and gas (vapor) forms.

The atmosphere (AT - MUH - SFEER) is the layer of gases surrounding our planet. This is the air we breathe! It also protects us from the radiation and heat from the sun.

The biosphere (BI - O - SFEER) is all living things on the earth, on land or in water.

The lithosphere (LITH - O - SFEER) is the rocky layer of the earth's surface. It consists of the crust and a part of the mantle.

Do you remember?

What are the four
main layers of the earth?

Which section is the
largest part of the earth?

What are the names
of the four spheres of the earth?

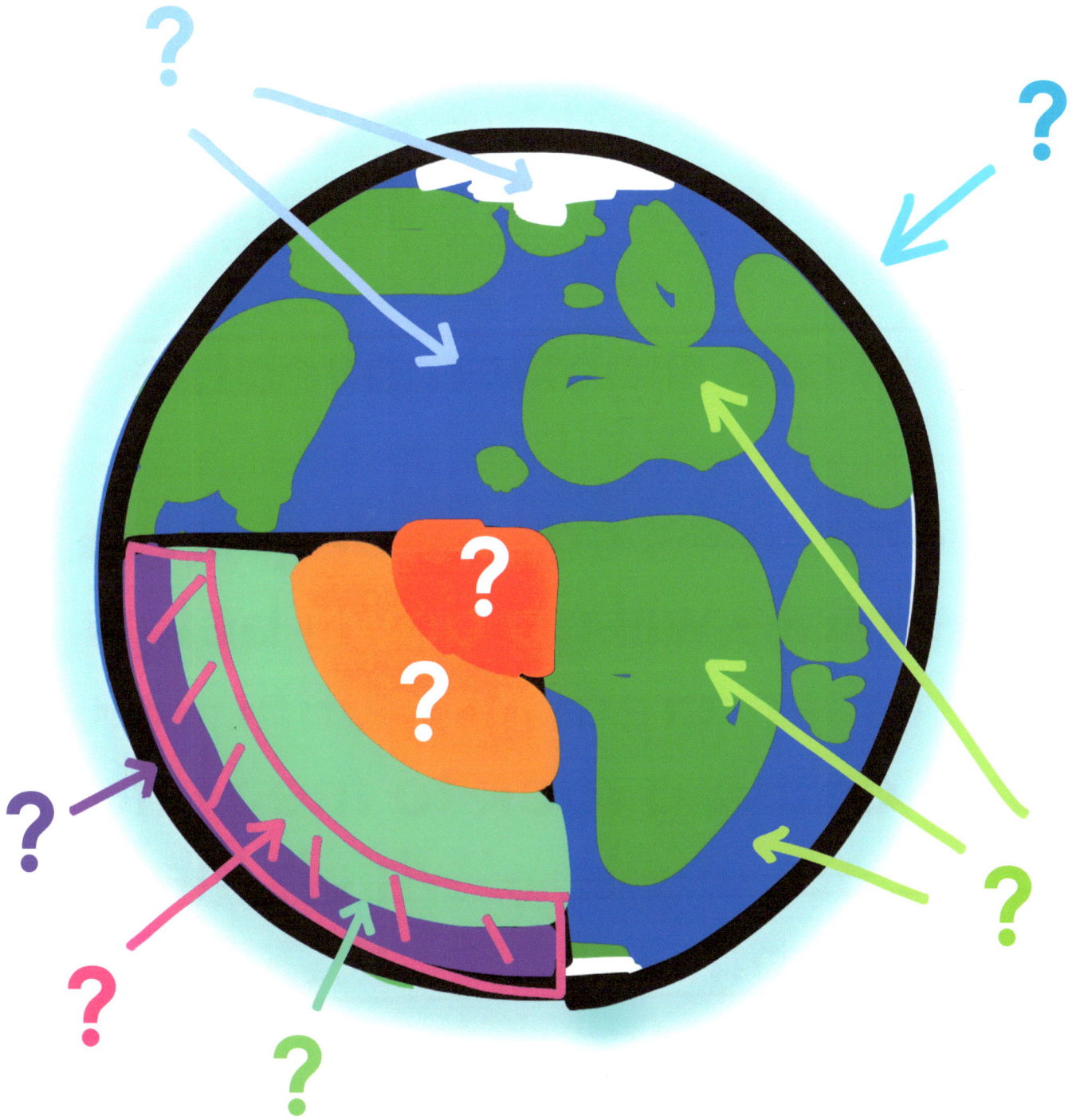

Excellent!

Tectonic Plates

Tectonic plates (TEK-TON-IK PLAYTS) are giant pieces of the earth's crust that are part of the lithosphere.

Plates are slightly moveable.

When plates converge (KUN - VERJ), one plate will go down below the other, creating earthquakes and causing rock to melt into magma (MAG - MUH), which then erupts from volcanoes.
(VOL - KAN - OZ)

This is an example of two oceanic plates converging.

When 2 oceanic plates converge, a very deep trench is formed in the ocean floor and a chain of volcanic (VOL - KAN - IK) islands will form.

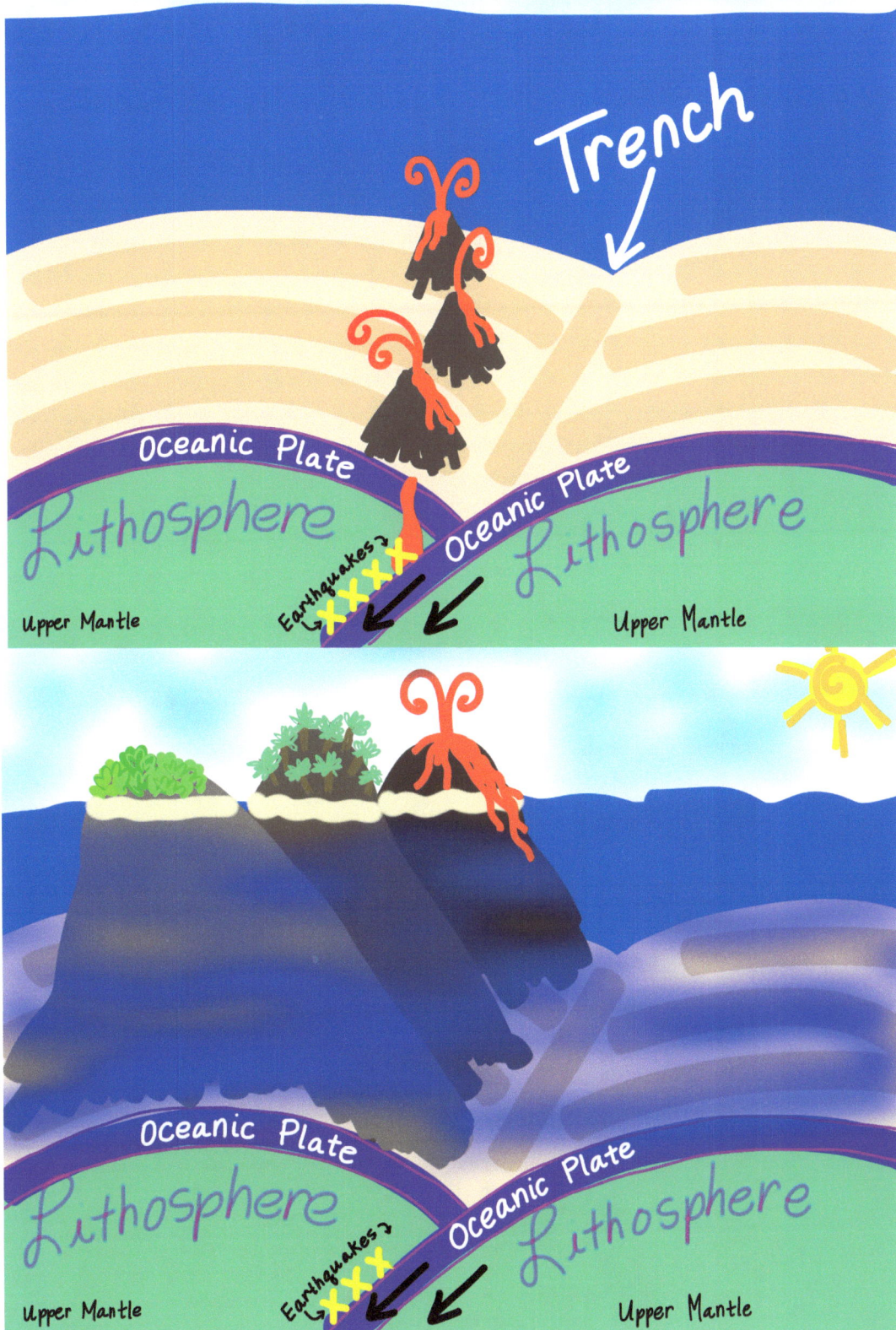

Volcano

Volcanoes are mostly located where tectonic plates meet.

Ash Cloud

Crater
Vent

Lava

Ash

Conduit

Crust

Magma

Mantle

Extremely hot liquid-rock under earth's surface is called magma.

Pressure causes magma to move up through the pipe-like conduit (KON - DU - IT), and out the <u>vent</u> through the <u>crater</u>.

When magma exits the volcano, it is called *lava*.

Lava flows down the surface of the volcano, then ash from the ash cloud layers on top of the *lava*.

This pattern continues as the volcano gets larger.

Landforms

How many of these landforms can you name?

1
2
3
4
5
6
7
8
9
10

11

12

13

14

15

16

17

18

Mountain
MOUN-TUN

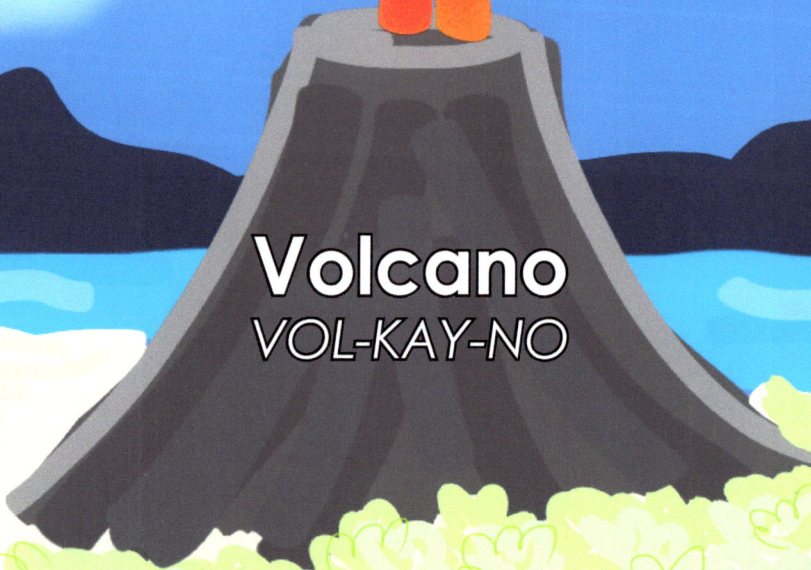

Volcano
VOL-KAY-NO

Lake
LAYK

Butte
BYOOT

Plateau
PLA-TOE

Mesa
MAY-SUH

Strait
STRAYT

Cape
KAYP

Islands *I-LUNDZ*

Harbor
HAR-BR

Glacier
GLAY-SHUR

Hills
HILLZ

Waterfall
WAH-TR-FALL

River
RI-VR

Beach
BEECH

Delta
DEL-TUH

Ocean *O-SHUN*

Gulf *GULF*

Do you remember?

How many landforms can you remember?

What is magma?

What "pipe" does magma move through inside the volcano?

What two substances layer on top of one another, building up the volcano over time?

Where are volcanoes mostly located?

True or False

Magma is cold.

When two *plates* converge, *volcanoes* can be formed.

Earthquakes never occur where two *plates* converge.

VERY GOOD!

Rock

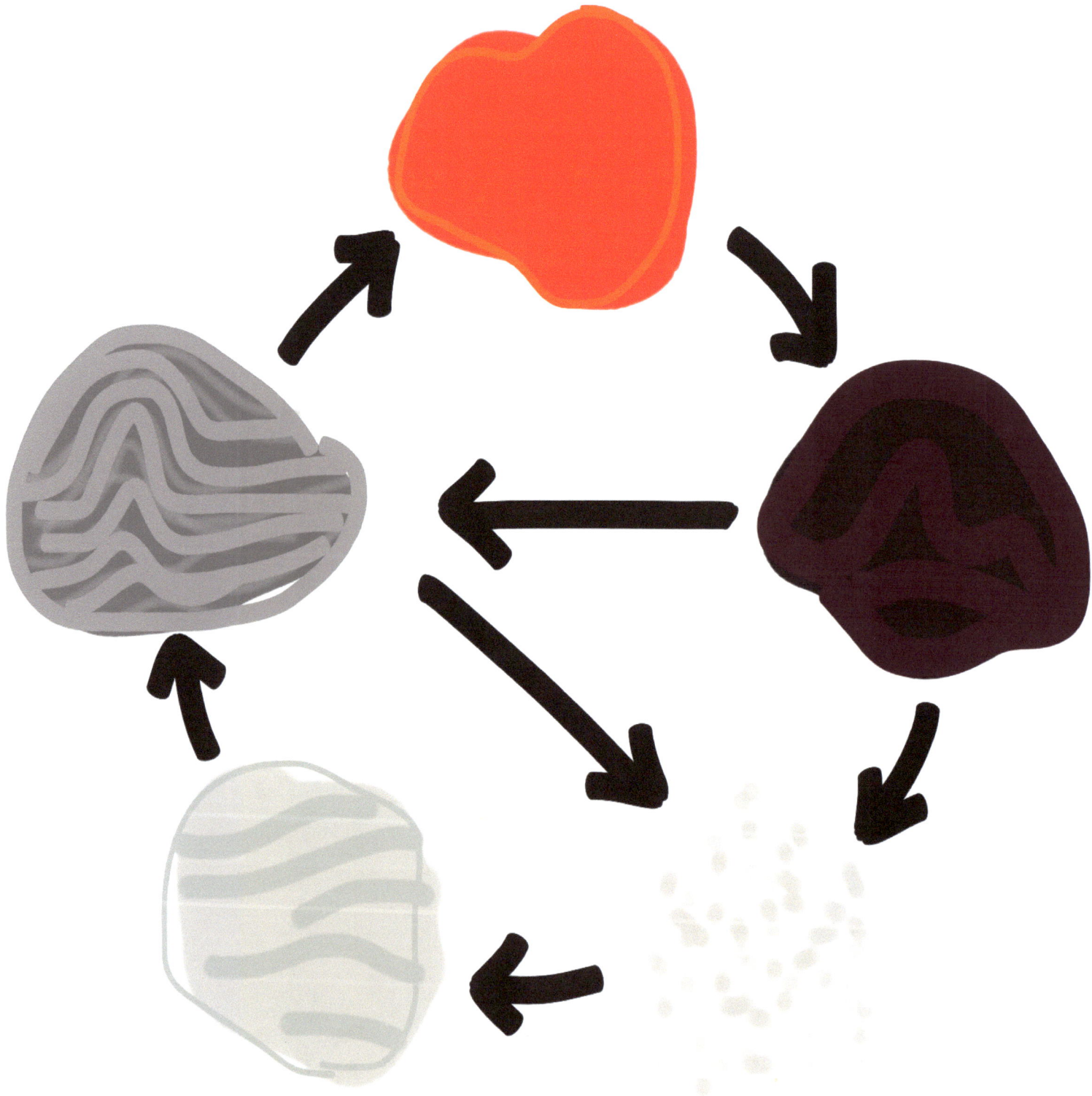

Cycle

There are three main types of rock on the earth.

Heat, pressure, weathering and erosion change the rocks into different forms.

This is the rock cycle diagram. It shows how the rocks are changed into each form.

There are three main types of rock: igneous, sedimentary and metamorphic.

Igneous rocks are formed when magma cools.

Weathering and erosion break down the rocks into small pieces (sediment). Wind and water move the sediment into piles.

The piles of sediment get covered and buried over time, solidifiying (SUH - LID - EH - FI - ING) and becoming sedimentary rock.

Igneous becomes sedimentary, and igneous can become metamorphic through heat + pressure.

Rock Cycle

Magma

melting

(cooling) Crystallization

Metamorphic Rock

heat and pressure

Igneous Rock

weathering deposition

weathering transportation deposition

heat and pressure

Sedimentary Rock

Sediment

lithification (cementation)

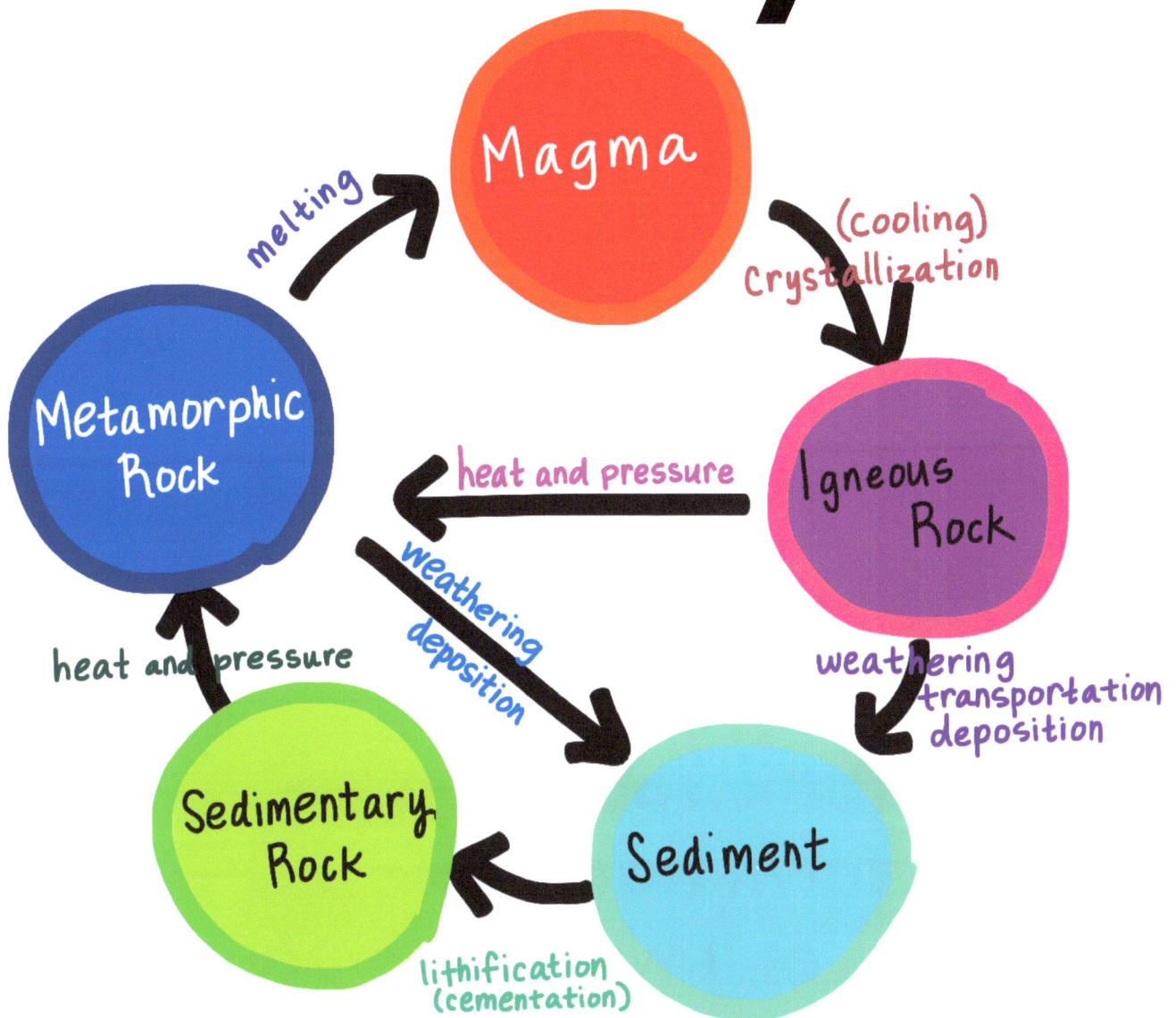

Igneous: IG - NEE - USS

Sediment: SED - EH - MINT

Sedimentary: SED - EH - MIN - TUH - REE

Metamorphic: MET - UH - MOR - FIK

Sedimentary rock will continue to be buried deeper into the Earth's crust. Heat + pressure changes sedimentary rock into metamorphic rock.

Sedimentary becomes metamorphic.

Metamorphic rock can be broken down again into sediment, or it will continue to be buried deeper into the Earth and melt into magma.

Metamorphic can become sediment or magma.

Rock Cycle

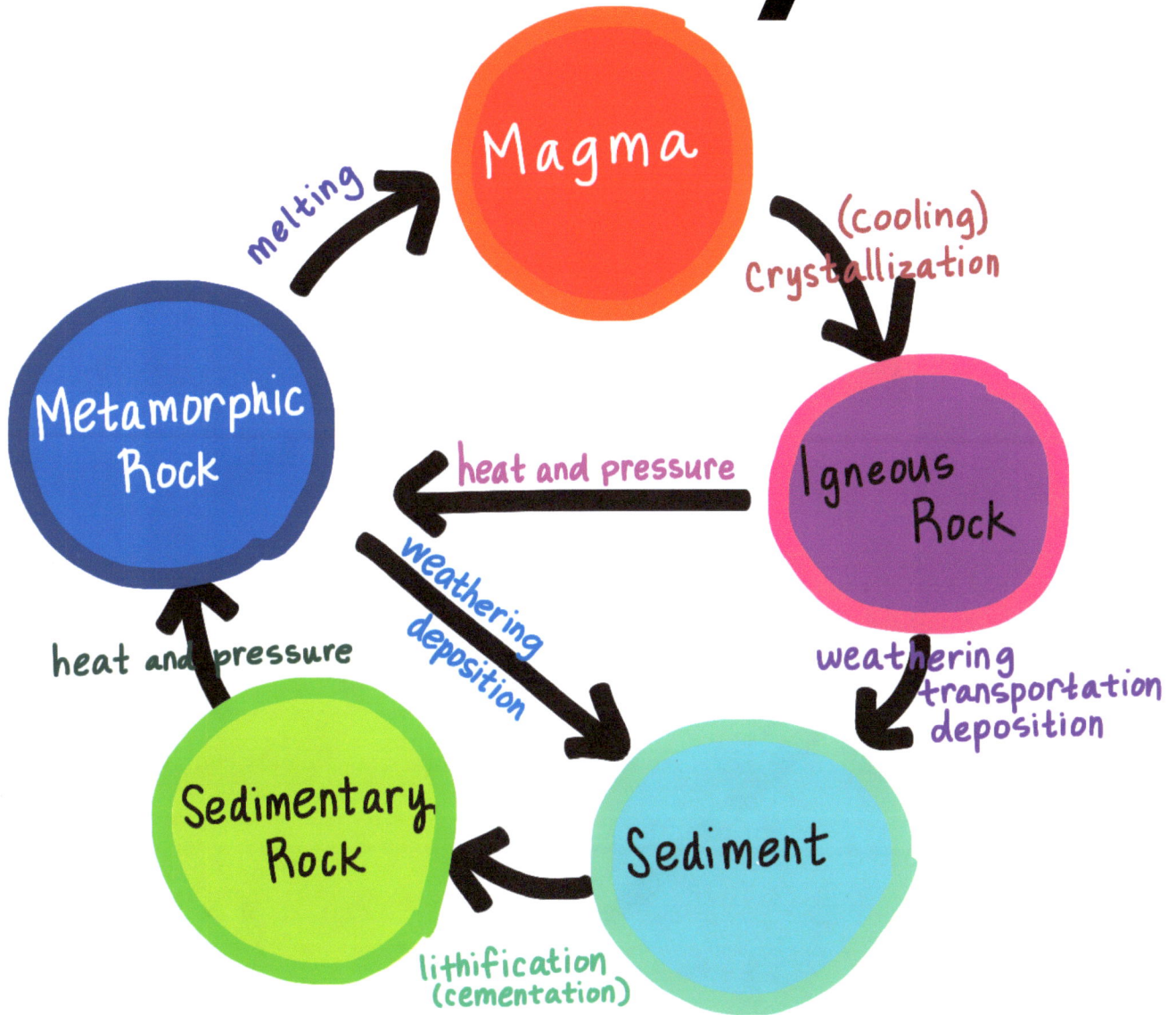

Magma

melting

(cooling)
Crystallization

Metamorphic
Rock

heat and pressure

Igneous
Rock

weathering
deposition

weathering
transportation
deposition

heat and pressure

Sedimentary
Rock

Sediment

lithification
(cementation)

*Practice saying the name of
each part of the rock cycle!*

Do you remember?

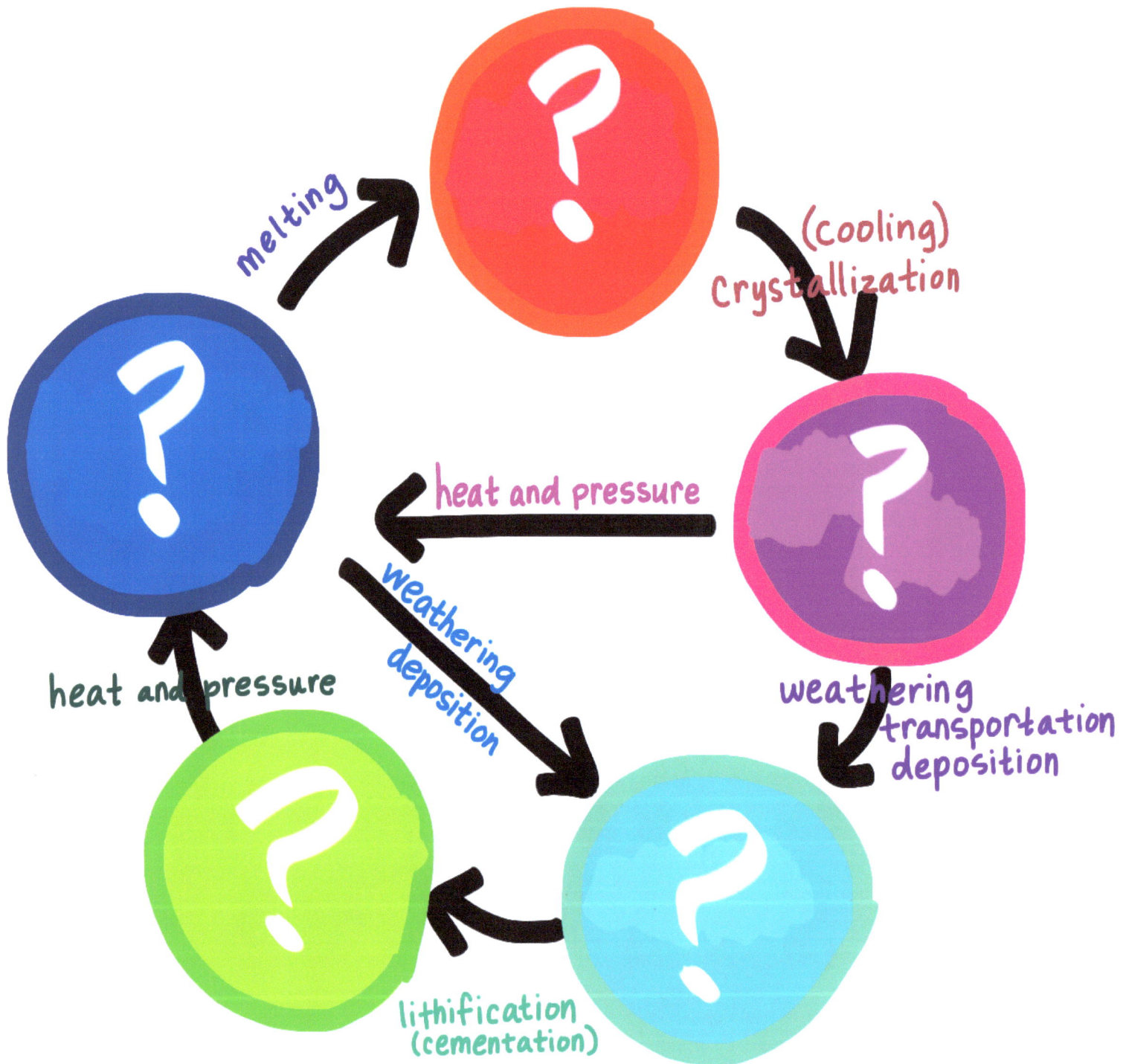

melting

(cooling)
Crystallization

heat and pressure

weathering
deposition

heat and pressure

weathering
transportation
deposition

lithification
(cementation)

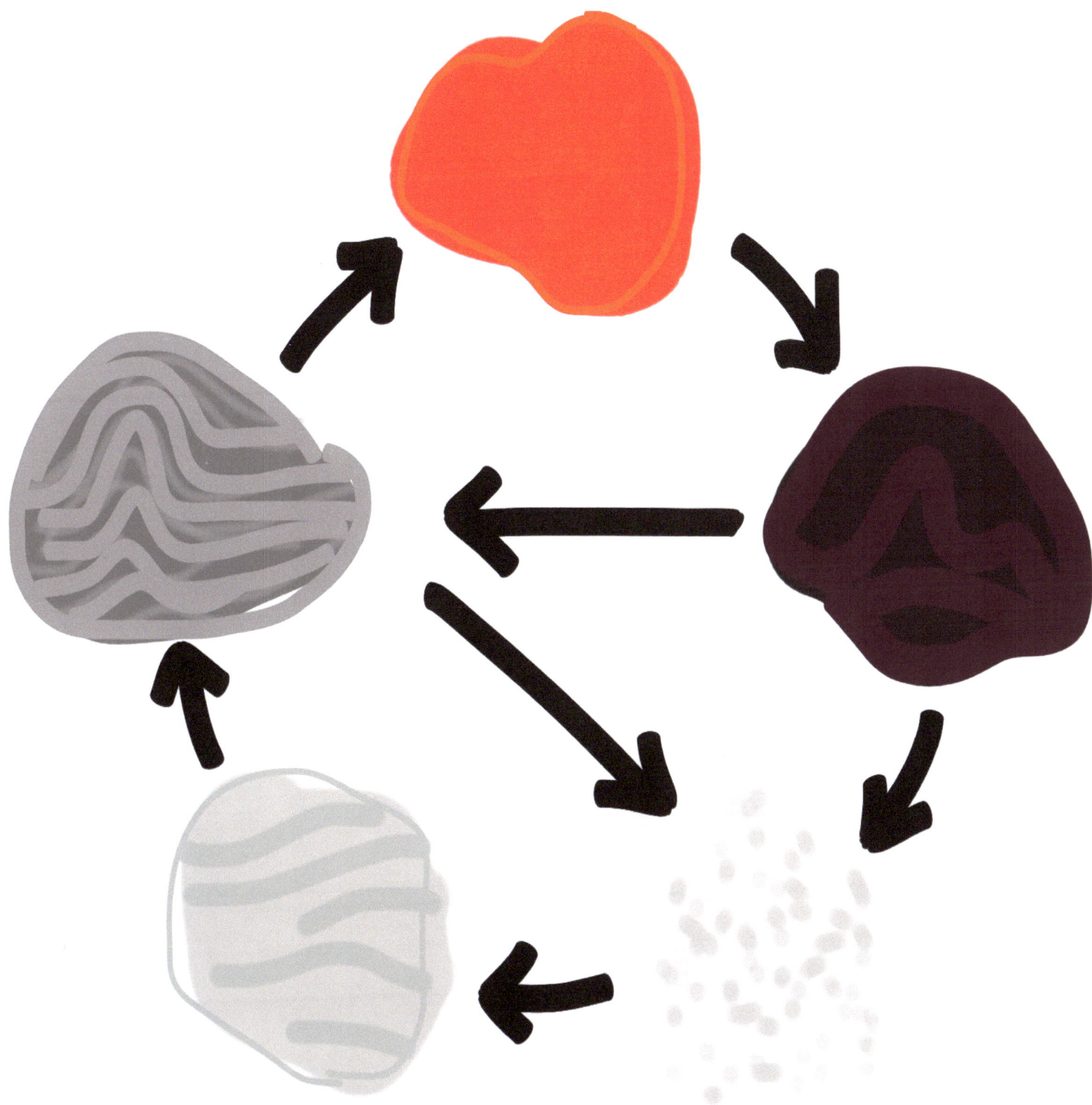

Well done!

Cloud
(KLOUD)

Precipitation
(PRE-SIP-EH-TA-SHUN)

Water Cycle

Percolation
(PUR-KO-LA-SHUN)

Aquifer
(AW-KWEH-FUR)

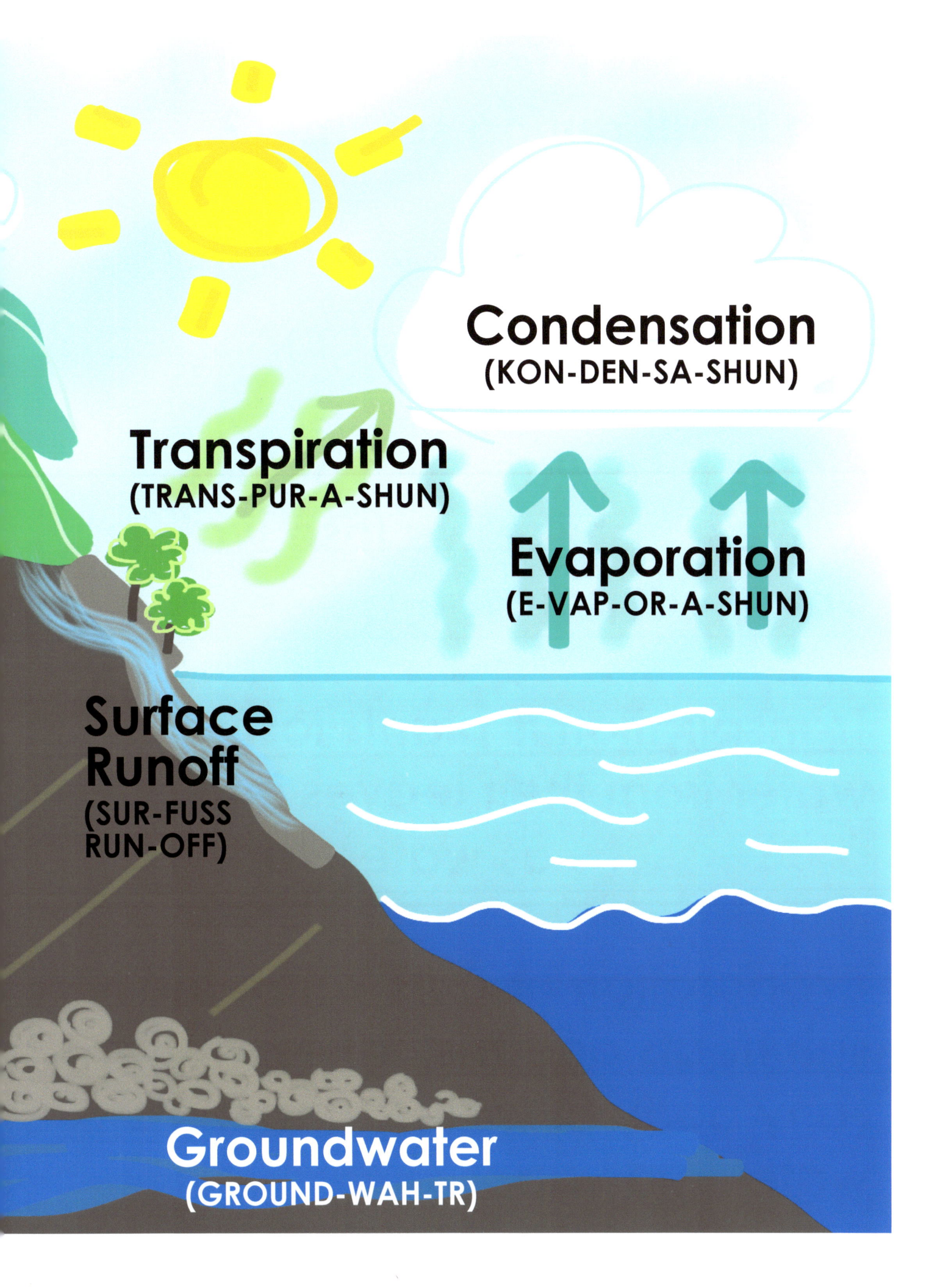

What does it feel like when the sun is out during summer?

Do you sweat?
Did you know that plants sweat?

Plants lose water out of their leaves, just like we lose water out of our pores.

Transpiration is plants losing water from their leaves into the atmosphere as water vapor.

Evaporation occurs when the sun heats oceans, lakes, rivers (any body of water) and turns water into vapor.

Water vapor goes into the atmosphere and gets very cold, causing it to become liquid water again in the form of clouds. This is the process of <u>condensation</u>.

(Condensation also occurs when you have a cold drink outside on a hot day)

When the cloud gets too heavy with water, <u>precipitation</u> occurs.

<u>Precipitation</u> is when water falls back to the surface of the earth as rain, sleet or snow.

After <u>precipitation</u> occurs, water enters the ground and goes through <u>percolation</u>.

<u>Percolation</u> is the movement of water through the ground (layers and layers of soil and rocks).

<u>Groundwater</u> contained in permeable (PUR - MEE - UH - BL) rock is called an <u>aquifer</u>.

Permeable means liquids and gases can move through it.

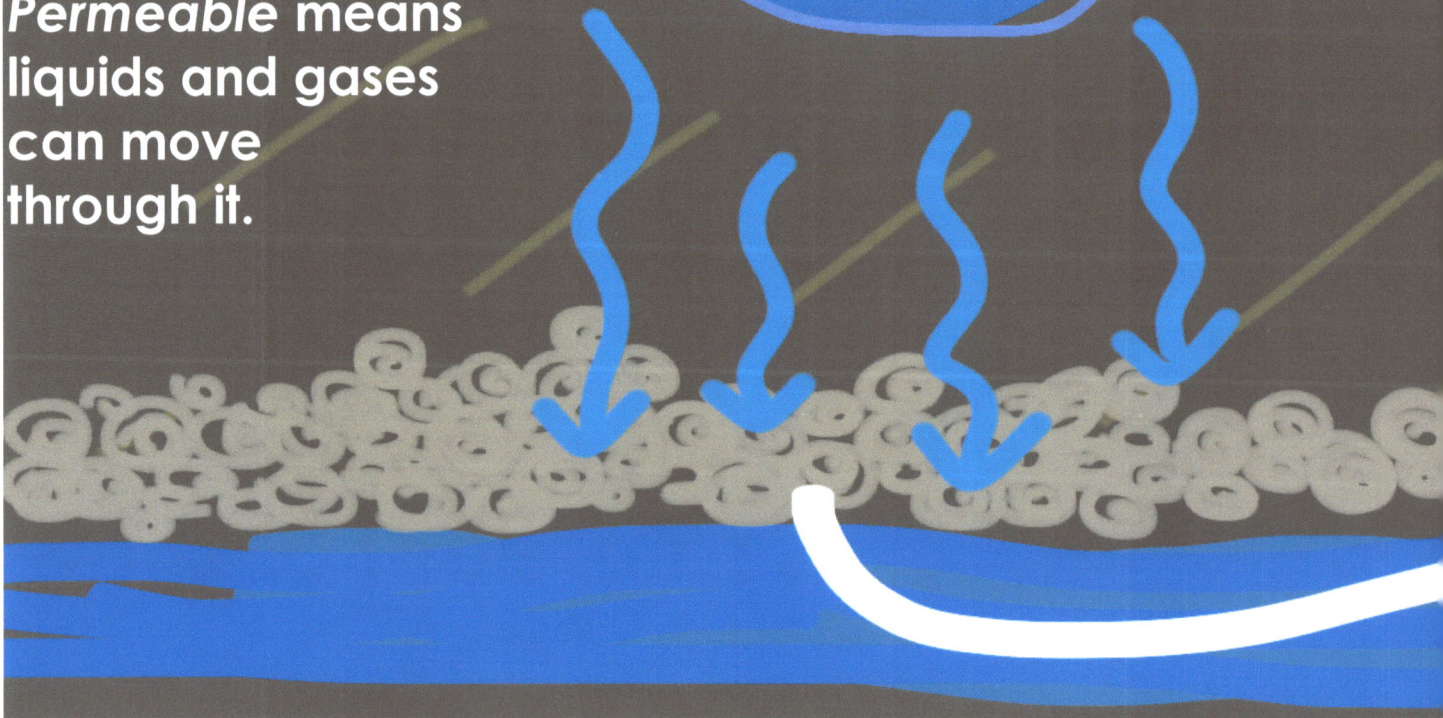

Aquifers provide water for us to drink. **Precipitation** and **surface runoff** goes into **aquifers**.

Chemicals and toxins can contaminate (KUN-TAM-IN-ATE) **aquifers**. We take care of the earth and our water supply by NOT littering or polluting on the surface where water is collected.

Do you remember?

Good Job!

Geology is the study of how the earth was formed, and what it is made of.

Earth is composed of four main layers: the inner core, the outer core, the mantle and the crust. The inner core can reach 5,000 degrees celsius!

The four spheres of the earth interact with each other: the hydrosphere, atmosphere, biosphere and lithosphere.

Tectonic plates are part of the earth's crust, and therefore part of the lithosphere.

Volcanoes form where tectonic plates meet.

When two tectonic plates converge, one plate goes below the other, creating earthquakes. The pressure causes magma to erupt from volcanoes. Ash and lava layer on top of each other, gradually making a larger and larger volcano.

There are many landforms on the earth that create a varied and beautiful landscape. How many landforms can you remember?

The rock cycle shows how the three main types of rock (igneous, sedimentary and metamorphic) change into different forms through heat, pressure, weathering, erosion.

Water is <u>evaporated</u> by heat from the sun, pulling water vapor into the atmosphere. Plants release water into the atmosphere through <u>transpiration</u>. As water vapor enters the atmosphere, it becomes cold, and the vapor becomes water again forming clouds. This is <u>condensation</u>. When the clouds become full of water, <u>precipitation</u> occurs, and water is returned to the surface by rain, sleet or snow.

Our drinking water comes from the surface of the earth! Protect our <u>aquifers</u> and water supply by not littering or polluting.
Congratulations, YOU ARE A GEOLOGIST!

Geology	Mountain	Igneous
Geologist	Lake	Sediment
Inner core	Butte	Sedimentary
Outer core	Plateau	Metamorphic
Mantle	Mesa	Solidifiying
Crust	Strait	Evaporation
Magma	Cape	Transpiration
Continental	Islands	Condensation
Oceanic	Harbor	Cloud
Hydropshere	Hills	Precipitation
Atmosphere	Glacier	Surface Runoff
Biosphere	Waterfall	Percolation
Lithosphere	River	Permeable
Tectonic plates	Delta	Aquifer
Converge	Beach	Contaminate
Volcano	Gulf	Groundwater
Lava	Ocean	
Conduit		
Vent		
Crater		

...and most important, protect your water supply!
NO LITTER, NO POLLUTION

www.ingramcontent.com/pod-product-compliance
Lightning Source LLC
Chambersburg PA
CBHW041547040426
42447CB00002B/79